GETTING TO E.Q. LIBRIUM

YVETTE BETHEL

Getting to E.Q. Librium
Activity Book

Graphic Design by Ray daSilva
Cover Design by Multimedia Mars
Cover Photo by ©iStockphoto/artSILENSE

Organizational Soul, Ltd.
P.O. Box N-511,
Nassau, Bahamas.
www.orgsoul.com

ISBN 978-0-578-09922-4

Printed in the United States of America
First Edition Printing 2012

CONTENTS

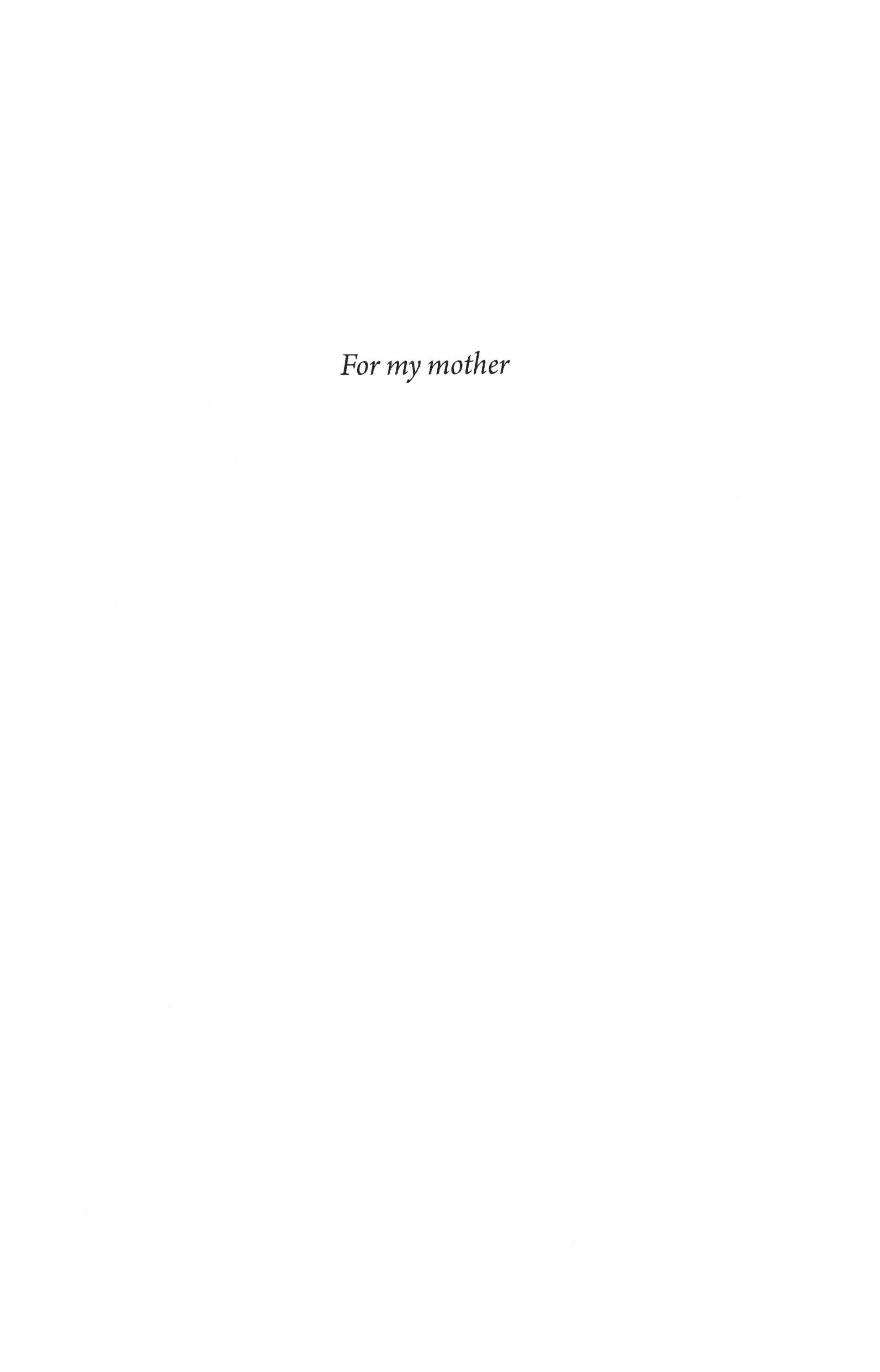

For my mother

PART ONE

DEVELOPING BASIC E.Q. SKILLS

Your activity book is a guide for a personal journey of E.Q. skill development. PART ONE focuses on helping you to build core emotional intelligence skills, setting the stage for PARTS TWO through THREE. Use the competency list in PART THREE to help you to develop answers to self-awareness questions and to assist you with your journaling.

What is E.Q. Librium?

AUTHOR Yvette Bethel coined the term *E.Q. Librium* to describe your ability to use your Emotional Quotient (E.Q.) to achieve balance in emotionally charged situations. *E.Q. Librium* is achieved when you are able to identify both your emotions and the emotions of others, and you can filter that information into a balanced, holistic, and self-regulated response.

When you build your capacity to balance your emotions internally, you can become a positive influence within a group. The more people in a group who can navigate their emotions, the more effective the group will be at communicating purposefully and respectfully, particularly when there are diverse personalities at play.

Achieving *E.Q. Librium* means you are attaining conscious personal and team emotional attunement. When in a state of *E.Q. Librium*, intentional strategies designed to circumvent emotional reactions are more easily implemented.

E.Q. Librium involves using emotional intelligence to bring emotional stability to a situation and presupposes that individuals and team members will experience a variety of emotions. The traits needed to achieve *E.Q. Librium* are integrity, self-management, curiosity, objectivity, and accountability, despite prevailing emotions.

Seeking *E.Q. Librium* in a team environment does not mean you will always find a solution that will make everyone happy. In fact, your decision may be profoundly unpopular. What it does mean is that leaders are equipped with the skills to listen with empathy, manage morale, make decisions that are uncluttered by emotion, and address the fears of the team. Additionally, leaders can facilitate multichannel flows of information so that relevant information continuously moves to and from the right people at the right times, and issues are addressed.

E.Q. Librium will help you to seek solutions to serve the greater good. In addition, because this approach may not be palatable to everyone affected by your decisions, it can help you to manage the fallout. In reality, maintaining *E.Q. Librium* is an art, and you may have to try several different strategies before finding one that brings the balance you seek.

Getting to E.Q. Librium is an introspective path to *E.Q. Librium*. Once you complete the activity book, you will be more aware of yourself and others. Take advantage of the list of Emotional Intelligence Competencies listed in Part Three of this activity book. The list is designed to help stimulate your ideas so you can set clearer objectives for your E.Q. development; it will be referenced throughout the activity book.

EMOTIONAL SELF-AWARENESS

THE term *emotional literacy* refers your ability to name your emotions when you are experiencing them, whether you are experiencing a single emotion or multiple emotions. Developing your emotional vocabulary will bring your emotions into focus and allow you to target specific emotions in your quest to build your emotional quotient.

Families of Emotion

- **Angry**: furious, outraged, resentful, annoyed, hostile, impatient, frustrated, entitled, jealous, unappreciated, disgust, contempt, unforgiving, irritated, rage, vengeful.
- **Loving**: accepting, friendly, trusting, kind, caring, infatuated, committed, appreciated, valued, forgiving, awe.
- **Ashamed**: guilty, remorseful, humiliated, rejected, embarrassed, insulted.

- **Fearful**: anxious, withdrawn, isolated, nervous, apprehensive, terrified, distrustful, insecure, overwhelmed, stressed, tense, uneasy, worried.
- **Happy**: happy, joyful, relieved, content, pleased, optimistic, hopeful, anticipating, cheerful, delighted, proud.
- **Sad**: Grieving, sorrowful, gloomy, hurt, miserable, disappointed, neglected, sympathetic, tired, despair.
- **Surprised**: Shocked, astonished, amazed.
- **Detached**: indifferent, apathetic, unfazed, unaffected, bored.

References: Plutchik, Robert & H. Kellerman Eds. (1980), *Emotion: Theory, research, and experience: Vol. 1. Theories of emotion,* (pp. 3–33), New York: Academic.

Parrott, W. (2001), Emotions in Social Psychology, Psychology Press, Philadelphia. "List of Emotions" Changing Minds web page, accessed September 2011. http://changingminds.org/explanations/emotions/basic%20emotions.htm

Using the families of emotions above:

List the full range of emotions you typically experience at work. Think about words you typically use that describe your emotions.

____

____

____

____

____

____

____

____

____

E.Q. Librium Tip

Building your ability to name your emotions will lead to your ability to detect what is going on with the people around you. This knowledge will help you to avoid unpleasant surprises.

Recognize Your Patterns

HERE is a list of emotional patterns. Use the following list to contemplate patterns that could be inhibiting you from going to the next level of E.Q. Librium:

- People pleasers
- Victims
- Blamers
- Always right
- Poor listening skills
- Hiding behind masks
- Bullying
- Control (Setting conditions for everyone else to follow)
- Denial
- Avoidance
- Lying
- Advice givers
- Defensive
- Competitive
- Angry
- Bitter
- Impatient
- Unforgiving
- Other________________________________

Now decide which emotional patterns you can manage differently, because when unchecked, these patterns can lead to unwanted interactions/outcomes.

Emotional Patterns I Would Like to Manage Differently	I Know I Am Experiencing This Emotional Pattern When I Am:	
	Thinking	Doing

Patterns of behavior can emerge in the form of unconscious verbal and/or non-verbal reactions. Non-verbal responses include your body language, tone, and volume. In the workplace, emotional patterns may surface immediately or they can take a while to become evident.

Now take your list of emotional patterns and think about the emotion behind each pattern. How do your coworkers respond to you when you experience these emotions and display these patterns?

Negative/destructive responses to your emotionally-driven behaviors are indicators of opportunities for improving your E.Q.

Blind Spots

You may not detect your pattern because it is a blind spot, and blind spots occur when you demonstrate behaviors that are undetectable to you (unconscious) and obvious to others. They can hinder your career development causing a feeling of frustration or stagnation. Blind spots are easily detected by others, because we are deceiving ourselves into overlooking our shortcomings. Whether the cause is arrogance or low self-awareness it will behoove you to identify your blind spots and actively correct them.

Sometimes coworkers may appear to respond positively to your negative patterns because of fear or tension, so they feed your blind spot. These coworkers may tell you what they think you want to hear so keep in mind your patterns may take a little longer to surface in the form of failed/delayed plans, passive aggression, or the lack of input from coworkers. Another complaint that may be an indicator of a blind spot is that you may feel like you always have to spoon-feed coworkers. Sometimes employees adopt this approach because they don't want to take risks; they may fear your emotional reactions.

Questions to help you to identify your blind spots:

Think about times when persons reacted extremely negatively or positively toward you, and you were not sure why the person reacted that way. What did you do to contribute to the reaction?

____

____

____

____

____

____

____

____

____

What are some of the things your coworkers say to you (about you) in jest? They may lack the courage to have a direct conversation with you so they hide behind friendly banter.

Reflect on how you react when you are criticized. Do you listen, do you try to explain or defend your position?

Think about how you react to bad news. Do you become emotional? Do you prefer to avoid responding? Do you respond appropriately? How do you think you are being perceived in this state?

Consider your strengths. Sometimes your strengths can become weaknesses or blind spots because of how you misuse or abuse them. How do your coworkers respond when you overuse your strengths?

When you are in a heightened state of emotion/stress you are sometimes only aware of your emotions, not the effect you are having on others. Take time to consider the impact you have on others while in this state.

We are sometimes unaware of the non-verbal cues we receive because we are so absorbed in our own situations. Pay attention to your coworkers' body language to determine whether they are reacting negatively to you.

If you trust a coworker, ask for feedback related to your strengths and your weaknesses. Who should you approach and how should you approach him or her?

The following exercise is designed to take the emotional pattern exercise one step further, integrating blind-spot information. It will help you to become aware of how coworkers respond to your perceivable and blind patterns and to decide what you will do to correct patterns that are not optimal for you. Hint for identifying blind patterns: start by listing how employees respond to you suboptimally.

Blind Emotional Patterns I Would Like to Change	How Coworkers Respond to Me When I Display This Emotional Pattern	Conscious Patterns I Will Adopt to Replace the Blind Patterns

Emotional Triggers

While emotional triggers can be positive, they can be negative pressure points that, when activated, lead to negative reactions that are unbridled, uncontemplated, and based purely on impulse. These responses are hard-wired over years of making associations and reacting.

There are behaviors and situations that trigger an emotion within you whenever you encounter them. Examples of behaviors that can trigger a negative emotional reaction within you can range from:

- Loud, obnoxious behavior
- Incompetence
- Injustice/unfairness
- Condescension
- Profanity
- Lies, half-truths, spin
- Idiosyncrasies of others
- Boundary encroachment
- A lack of information/communication

Identify your emotional triggers in the list above.

It is useful to identify your emotional triggers so you can choose to respond instead of allowing your emotions to cause you to knee-jerk into a destructive pattern. Behaviors and situations that trigger a negative emotion for you are:

____

____

____

____

____

____

What can you do when your emotional triggers are activated? Here are samples of emotionally-competent responses to emotional triggers. Select the tools you feel most comfortable using.

- Walk away from the situation (depending on the situation)
- Stop and think
- Breathe deeply
- Reframe the situation (manage my thoughts)
- Set boundaries (say "no")
- Exercise
- Listen to Music
- Relaxation
- Talk to an objective person you trust to gain insight
- Other______________________________

E.Q. Librium Tip

Self-awareness and self-regulation are critical ingredients for emotionally intelligent responses and can lead to harmony.

Diffusing Emotion

Using the list of emotional triggers above, take the time to itemize the emotions you need to frequently diffuse within yourself and the emotional-diffusion tools that work best for you.

Emotion	Tools I Can Use to Diffuse the Emotion

Self-Awareness Notes:

How are you truly perceived by others? Are you perceived as balanced, emotional, or controlling? What do you plan to do differently to enhance your behavior?

Reframing Model

THE reframing model is useful for helping you to diffuse heightened emotion and reworking emotional patterns.

Understand My Emotion(s)	Opportunities to Change My Understanding and Response	Respond
Identify my emotions and the thoughts behind them.	How can I use this situation to develop myself?	How do I respond, taking my goals for the situation into consideration?
Am I willing to release emotions that do not serve me or the situation? If so, what is the best tool given the circumstances?	How does my preferred response affect my brand within my corporate and external networks?	How do I determine the right timing and implement a plan of action?
Identify my goals for the situation and understand the consequences of my actions. Ask myself whether I want to maintain relationships or trust. Can I use a response that will position me for future leverage? How does my decision affect the power dynamics?	What are the new behaviors I need to demonstrate to impact the situation?	How do I align all of my communication (verbal and non-verbal)? How do I ensure that I am listening and connecting?
Is this my problem or should someone else take ownership?	Do I have a mentor or coach who can help me analyze the situation?	How do I sustain the behaviors over time?
Consciously transform my negative thoughts so I can respond differently.	Do I need to modify my goals for the outcome?	How do I evaluate the solutions?

Use the questions in the reframing model to reframe a difficult situation.

E.Q. Librium Tip

Reframing is most difficult when you are in an emotional state. However, this is sometimes the only time to reframe, because the situation demands an immediate response. Reframing is much easier said than done.

Body Language Awareness

THERE are times when you may monitor what you say, but your emotions come through because of unregulated body language. The table below lists examples of body language that can trigger emotions in others and derail communication.

Body Language to Avoid	What It Can Signify
Rolling eyes	Impatience/anger
Not making eye contact	Fear, insecurity, something to hide (liar)
Fidgeting/tapping	Nervous, insecure
Frowning	Displeased, disappointed, angry

Body Language to Avoid	What It Can Signify
Closed body posture like folded arms	Defensive/angry
Checking the time	Impatient, bored
Working on an electronic device/phone while in a conversation	Impatient, bored, anxious
Yawning	Bored, tired
Opening your mouth as if to speak when someone else is speaking	Impatient, bored
Scowling	Displeased
A blank stare	Shock, displeasure
Inappropriate laughter or smiles	Judgment, nervous

Now it is time for you to identify the body language you exhibit and how it impedes constructive communication—and ultimately healthy work relationships.

____

____

____

Self-Awareness Notes:

How is your non-verbal behavior truly perceived by others? What do you plan to do differently?

____

____

____

____

WATCH YOUR WORDS

ANOTHER pattern you can take time to more clearly recognize is your tendency to use self-limiting, emotional statements. The words you consciously or subconsciously repeat become affirmations that help to perpetuate undesired emotional states. So as part of your E.Q. building process it is important for you to become aware of words you typically repeat, because you may be affirming a state that is not serving you. Here are a few examples of statements you need to watch.

- "I am sick and tired."
- "I am frustrated."
- "I don't care."
- "I don't trust anyone."
- "I can't ..." (i.e. I can't take this anymore; I can't stand ...)
- "I am stressed out."

What are some of the statements you use in your everyday interactions that you need to monitor? Which affirmations will you use to replace them?

Common Negative Affirmations	Replacement Affirmations

Self-Awareness Notes:

How are your non-verbal responses truly perceived by others? (i.e. How would you perceive others with similar language?) What do you plan to do differently?

CONSEQUENTIAL AWARENESS

WE all experience the consequences of our actions whether or not the consequences are positive. Sometimes consequences cause you to perceive yourself as a victim, because you are not understanding or acknowledging the part you played as the architect of your circumstances. Instead of unconscious victimhood, it helps if you are aware of how your decisions and responses affect you and others. For instance, if emotion is behind your unhealthy assumptions or understanding of the facts and you are unconscious about your patterns of behavior, you will find it difficult to extract yourself from a victim state. Below is a model of consequential thinking that illustrates how you can deliberately determine the consequences of your actions.

Consequential Analysis Model

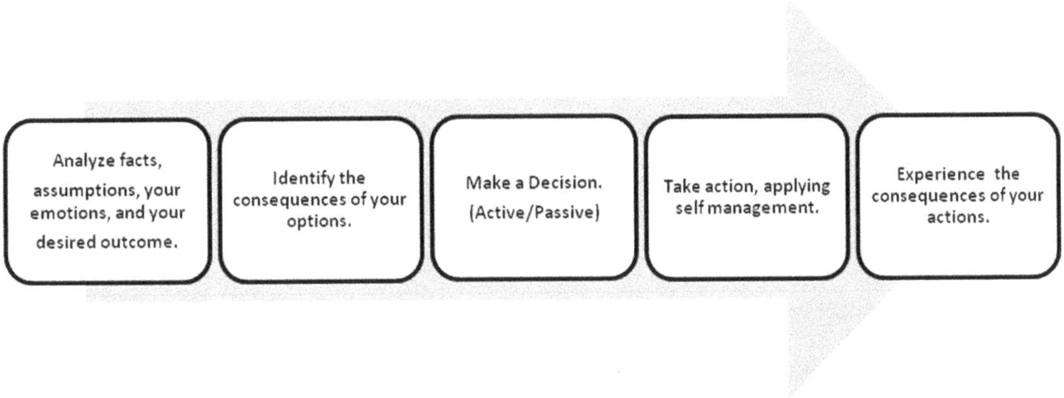

Analyze facts, assumptions, your emotions, and your desired outcome.

Identify the consequences of your options.

Make a Decision. (Active/Passive)

Take action, applying self management.

Experience the consequences of your actions.

An Example of How to Use the Consequential Thinking Model

Fact: My doctor told me I need to get in shape because of health risks.

Thought/Emotion: I am uncomfortable going to the gym because I am self-conscious about my body. I want to be held accountable, though, because it is hard to sustain my drive for exercise if I exercise at home.

Consequential Options: I can go to the gym despite my discomfort. (Will I be able to sustain this?) I can purchase a DVD and exercise at home. (Will I be able to sustain this?) I can work out with a trainer at home or at a venue other than a gym. (Can I afford this option?)

Critical Thinking: If I don't go to the gym I won't meet my personal fitness goals. I am not willing to accept the consequences of not exercising, so in what other way can I meet my goals if I don't go to the gym?

Self-management/decision: I will work out with a trainer at home until I build my confidence related to going to the gym.

Consequences: I will overcome my discomfort with getting started so that I can achieve my goals.

> **E.Q. Librium Tip**
> Indecision is a decision to maintain your current conditions.

Use the process above to explore the consequences of a decision you would like to make or the consequences of a decision you already made:

____

____

____

____

____

____

____

____

____

____

____

____

Tips for Identifying Consequences of Your Actions

- Identify intended positive consequences

____

____

- Identify intended negative consequences

____

____

- Identify unintended positive consequences

____

____

- Identify unintended negative consequences

____

____

- What can you do differently to convert an undesired (existing or potential) outcome to a desired outcome?

____

____

- Is your action an unconscious pattern that needs to change? If so, what can you do differently?

____

____

Self-Awareness Notes:

What typically happens when you don't fully explore the possible consequences of your actions? What do you plan to do differently to enhance your behavior?

INTRINSIC MOTIVATION AND INITIATIVE

YOUR motivation is based on your system of values. If you value what other people think more than your own needs and values, you are extrinsically motivated. Intrinsic motivation is directly linked to your internal value system, which drives your decisions. You may value power, status, relationships, honor, integrity, purpose, independence, or your goals. No matter what you value, if you are intrinsically motivated, your internal compass will cause you to contemplate your values when making decisions.

Rank Your Top Ten Values

One way to determine the source of your motivation is to identify your top-ten values. Keep in mind that there are times when you maintain values in a particular order of priority. Depending on the situation, the hierarchy of your values may change. The list below is composed of both extrinsic and intrinsic values. Review the list below and rank your top-ten values.

Rank	Value	Rank	Value
	Stability		Variety
	Independence		Excitement
	Creativity		Freedom
	Routine		Affiliation
	Team player		Recognition
	Security		Home/family life
	Money		What others think about you
	Constancy		Leading others
	Self development		Spirituality
	Helping others		Service
	Professional competence		Safety
	Status		Education
	Meaningful work		Health/wellness
	Power		Integrity and truth
	Family and friends		Giving (charity, church etc.)
	Intellectual status (Expertise in your field)		Loyalty
	Mental challenge and growth		Balance of work and life
	Having a positive impact on others		Stress-free/pressure-free environment
	Glamour		Authority to make and execute decisions
	Adventure and excitement		Variety

Rank	Value	Rank	Value
	Positive work relationships		Professional advancement opportunities
	Privacy		Efficiency
	Beauty		Boldness
	Peace		Love
	Perfection		Respect
	Goal achievement		Progress
	Knowledge		Experiences
	Responsibility		Other___________

Which of your top-ten values are intrinsically motivated? Which ones are motivated by what others think you should do?

____

____

____

____

____

Test Your Situational Motivation

Describe a situation that requires you to consider your values. (Select a current situation.)

____

____

____

Create a value hierarchy related to the situation by listing your top-five values as they relate to this situation.

0 - Not at all

5 - Somewhat

10 - Very

Rank	Important Values	How Well Am I Applying the Value To the Problem/Situation?
1		
2		
3		
4		
5		

How is this list the same or different than your top–ten list?

What did you decide to do?

Is your decision aligned with your top values? If not, which values are more aligned with your decision, and why are these values the only ones you factored into the decision?

Are there external parties or dynamics influencing your decision that should not be integrated into the decision-making process? If so, why?

Are there external parties or dynamics influencing your decision that should be integrated into the decision making process? If so, why?

Take a second look at the top-five values driving your decision. Are they the right values? If not, what should the primary driver(s) be?

What is your plan of action for enhancing your situational motivation?

Motivating Others

It is not possible to motivate intrinsically-motivated coworkers unless your agenda is aligned with theirs. It will help if you can identify their primary intrinsic motivators and plan your recognition efforts to address your coworkers' intrinsic motivators.

When recognizing others, be sure you are recognizing the behaviors you prefer and not inadvertently recognizing undesired behaviors. For instance, some leaders speak about teamwork but reward competition.

As a reflective exercise, think about someone you would like to motivate at work. You may want to influence that person to work with you, to perform in his/her role, to work with others, or do something else. Be sure you are influencing and not imposing your will on the person.

Self-Awareness Notes:

Are you typically intrinsically or extrinsically motivated? (i.e. How would you perceive persons who are extrinsically and intrinsically motivated?) What do you plan to do differently to improve your level of intrinsic motivation in all areas of your life?

Initiative

Initiative refers to your internal drive or predisposition to seek and perform duties or tasks without being asked or mandated. Initiative refers to your ability to use your creativity, insight, and problem-solving skills to recognize opportunities to close gaps. For example:

- Some persons take initiative to complete tasks that no-one else enjoys/everyone avoids.
- Initiative can be related to identifying ways to create more effective and/or efficient processes.
- Initiative can also occur when there is potential for conflict that is averted by managing relationships skillfully.
- Initiative can occur in the face of change when you understand the positive implications of a change and you become an agent of change without being asked. This also requires intrinsic motivation because many change initiatives are challenged by resistors.
- You can also use initiative to take an unpopular stand because of your values. You are not influenced by others; you are able to stand your ground, even if it means being ostracized.
- Perseverance is necessary because there may be persons or situations that will test your resolve.

One way to reframe in order to overcome entitlement or other initiative-destroying attitudes that inhibit you from going the extra mile is to attempt to see past the external presentation of a problem and seek the opportunities in the situation. Another way to reframe is to stop taking business decisions personally.

Understand that taking initiative could venture into the realm of taking on someone else's responsibility. In a healthy, balanced environment the reasons for this may be justifiable, however, in a dysfunctional environment your predisposition toward taking initiative may end up being used inappropriately. This is not an excuse to stop taking initiative but it is an opportunity to seek balance.

Always remember that taking initiative allows you to develop in areas that you may not have been given an opportunity to explore in normal circumstances. You can frame initiative as a developmental tool that can provide you with exposure and a chance to hone your skills based on your personal career goals.

In what ways do you take initiative at work?

In what ways do you avoid taking initiative at work?

Are there additional ways you can take initiative? If yes, what can you do differently? How can you reframe the situation?

E.Q. Librium Tip

Move to efficacy: Efficacy is the ability to rely on yourself to drive a desired result. It is directly linked to intrinsic motivation, because once you are intrinsically motivated you can persevere toward your goals without being influenced by the contradicting opinions of others.

OPTIMISM

OPTIMISM signifies a state of self-empowerment can lead to perseverance. Optimists believe that they are empowered and have control and choices. They view perceivably negative situations as temporary. Pessimists are inflexible and perceive the world as being out-of-control. Pessimists view difficult situations as never-ending, and they see themselves as victims of circumstances. To shift from pessimism to optimism, here is a process you can use.

Shifting from Pessimism to Optimism

Introspection	
Select a situation about which you feel pessimistic.	
What do you feel is out of your control?	
How can you bring that circumstance within your control?	
Now focus on the positive	
How can you circumvent your emotions and focus on the facts?	
Identify the (possible) benefits of the situation.	
What are alternative, empowering actions you can take?	
What are the consequences of acting on your empowered alternatives?	
How can you sustain optimism in similar circumstances in the future?	

12 Tips for Improving Your Optimism

1. Be realistic.
2. Be authentic.
3. Be a positive thinker; develop your ability to perceive the opportunity in each situation.
4. Find your purpose and do what you can to make it into a reality. When you are passionate about what you do, your perspective changes.
5. Reduce your stress levels.
6. Find a way to focus on solutions.
7. Forgive. Let go of perceived injustices.
8. Release your victim mentality.

9. Don't allow others to affect your optimism. Use your intrinsic motivation to remain hopeful.
10. Accept your shortcomings.
11. Express gratitude.
12. Occupy yourself with positive activities and with people who bring out the best in you.

Self-Awareness Notes:

Do you consider yourself to be optimistic or pessimistic? Why? What behaviors do you observe in others do you perceive as optimistic? Which behaviors in others do you perceive as pessimistic? What do you plan to do differently to transform your undesired behavior?

____

____

____

____

____

____

____

____

____

____

E.Q. Librium Tip

There is a line between optimism and delusion. Optimism involves being in a state of empowerment; delusion is a false belief that is held with absolute certainty despite evidence to the contrary. Understand the difference between the two, because delusions are blind spots that can lead to unpleasant surprises.

EMPATHY

EMPATHY refers to your ability to demonstrate compassion and build relationships based on your ability to put yourself in another person's shoes. It is an authentic experience that can lead to connectivity and trust.

Are you demonstrating empathy?

We are sometimes so entrenched in our personal reality/drama that we are incapable of connecting and expressing compassion for others. You can use the list below as a resource for guidance as to how you can demonstrate empathy. Select the behaviors that apply to you:

Behaviors That Demonstrate Empathy		Behaviors That Demonstrate a Lack of Empathy	
	Using words that capture the speaker's emotion. Use them to acknowledge the feelings of the speaker.		Launching into your own story, not listening to the speaker.
	Empathetic listening occurs when your words, body language, tone, and volume are aligned. You are controlling the urge to speak.		Give advice or lecture the speaker.
	Perceiving the situation from the speaker's point of view.		Mirroring the emotion of the speaker. Permitting emotional contagion that is not constructive.
	Avoiding being drawn into someone else's emotional experience, yet demonstrating an understanding of their emotion.		Changing the subject pre-maturely.
	Responding with authenticity and connection to the speaker.		Hurling insults (condescension, blame, etc.)
	Demonstrating self-awareness and self-management.		Avoiding making comments about the situation.
	Diffusing your emotions and the emotions of others.		Other
	Being non-judgmental.		
	Understanding what people want/ need.		
	Being sensitive to differences.		
	Other		

What can you do to change your behaviors that lack empathy to ones that demonstrate empathy and connection?

Self-Awareness Notes:

How empathetic are you? How do you connect with people authentically so they can tell you what they really think/feel? How would you perceive others who lack empathetic behavior?

E.Q. Librium Tip

Empathy is essential to your ability to connect. So are authenticity, humility, and integrity.

PART TWO

PRACTICAL APPLICATION OF E.Q. AT WORK

PART TWO is designed to help you to apply your emotional intelligence skills to everyday workplace situations.

Conflict Resolution

CONFLICT is a natural part of workplace-relationship dynamics. As an emotionally intelligent employee, you recognize that conflict can be constructive and that it should not be feared. You recognize that various conflict-resolution strategies are effective, and you are willing to apply a strategy to bring balance to the team dynamic.

The following questions are designed to guide you in taking steps to proactively understand and resolve conflict in any circumstance. Ask yourself:

What is the conflict? How am I defining the dynamics of the conflict? Is there another possible definition? Is the conflict obvious or is it subtle?

What is the root cause of the conflict? If you are unaware, do some investigative work that will not escalate the conflict. Don't rule yourself out as a possible primary source.

If the conflict is subtle or latent, what are the symptoms? Once you identify the symptoms, (body language, a change in power/relationship dynamics, etc.) then do some investigative work to find the root cause(s) without escalating the conflict.

Define your emotions related to the conflict and how you will reframe them to ensure your objectivity in the process.

____

____

____

____

____

____

For the situation you chose, which conflict resolution strategy/ies and tactics will you use and why?

- Find a way to diffuse the emotion
- Emotional intelligence
- Timing
- Stand your ground and refuse to give in
- Work with the team to find a solution together
- Avoid the problem, stay out of it
- Leverage the conflict, giving in order to achieve another goal
- Compromise
- Negotiation
- Mediation
- Other ______________________________

____

____

____

____

____

____

____

____

____

____

For the situation you chose to explore what are the possible consequences of your preferred strategy? Answer the following questions.

- What are the potential consequences of the strategy?
- Is it important for you to preserve relationships?
- How will you be affected by your strategy?
- Who are the stakeholders in this conflict?
- How will the stakeholders be affected by your strategy?
- How will interpersonal dynamics change? (Will power structures shift? If so, who will be negatively/positively impacted?)
- How will this choice affect your results?
- If the preferred strategy will (possibly) impair team trust, is it worth the sacrifice? If so, how will you rebuild trust?
- What do you want to get out of the conflict? Does your goal serve you only or the team? Should it?

____

____

CONFRONTATION

SOME people view confrontation as an approach to avoid, while others view it as invigorating. As a result, the emotions associated with confrontation can range from fear and anxiety to excitement. Regardless of the emotional response to confrontation, some use the words *confrontation* and *fighting* as synonyms; therefore, they choose a competitive style to resolve an issue. Others use the words *confrontation* and the phrase *constructive problem solving* as synonyms, and they choose a more collaborative, balanced approach.

Viewing confrontation from a consequential vantage point can lead you to review root causes of your responses to confrontation. For instance, some people avoid confrontation until it erupts into an aggressive exchange and as a result, they assign a negative connotation to confrontation. Others avoid conflict because it may expose a truth about themselves that they are unwilling to face. The opposite may be true of people who possess the skills of influence, negotiation, making distinctions, seeing from a *both/and* perspective, and managing their emotions. These skills may enable them to engage confrontation in a timely, confident, and self-regulated way.

You may be more confrontational in some circumstances than in others or you may be consistent with your confrontation style and strategy. How would you describe your approach to confrontation? What are the emotions behind your style? (if any)

Your timing can affect the outcome of a confrontation. If you confront a situation when you are emotionally charged, you will lack the self-regulation skills needed to listen and seek a solution. If you wait too long, trust can be compromised and it will be difficult to listen, negotiate, or influence a solution. Think about your timing as it relates to confronting situations and how it usually affects your results.

Behaviors to avoid when confronting a person or situation:

- Blame
- Low Blows/Personal attacks
- Manipulation
- Force
- Accusation
- Belittling
- Tactlessness
- Anger
- Minimizing
- Lecturing
- Scolding

Confrontation may or may not be associated with a conflict overlay. If your objective is to manage the situation without allowing conflict to permeate the circumstances, you can do this if you develop the appropriate skills. Skills that are useful for engaging confrontation constructively are listed below.

- Listening
- Using terms to illustrate that you understand the other person's point of view
- Identifying when you are saying the same thing in a different way
- Agreeing to disagree
- Reframing
- Understanding power dynamics
- Sticking to the facts
- Focusing on a solution
- Being direct
- Using "I" statements instead of "you" statements
- Goal setting

When considering the behaviors to avoid and the skills you can use to engage confrontation constructively, list the behaviors you can cease and the skills you can add to your constructive-confrontation arsenal.

____

____

____

____

____

____

____

Think about an opportunity you may have to confront a situation. Is it a situation with potential for conflict? What is your strategy to deal with that situation through confrontation?

____

____

____

____

____

____

E.Q. Librium Tip

Confrontation can be a positive experience if you are equipped with the right skills and the right attitude toward the exchange.

ENTITLEMENT VS. GRATITUDE

AN attitude of entitlement causes you to think primarily of yourself. Your capacity for fairness, optimism or compassion becomes difficult because you are locked in on your unmet needs. Entitlement attitudes make teamwork difficult, because it creates unhealthy dynamics such as, "every man for himself" or an "us and them" environment, where entitled employees block change attempts or teamwork.

When you feel entitled you perceive your rights as being infringed upon. When this happens your emotions can transform your attitude into anger or bitterness because of a sense of betrayal. Entitlement can happen because you have a distorted sense of what is fair or right, and as a result, you have a warped sense of what is due to you.

The right you perceive could be based on long tenure, loyalty, or hard work. Entitlement is not necessarily based on global principles of fairness, your results, or the policies of your organization.

An attitude of entitlement is a baseline for dysfunctional emotional patterns; therefore, it is useful for you to identify these attitudes so you can consciously work toward transforming them.

Here is a list of typical entitlement attitudes.

1. I have been employed longer so I am entitled to a raise.
2. I am loyal to the manager and I should be repaid for my loyalty.
3. I work hard so I should be rewarded.
4. I trained the new supervisor so I should be promoted.

When you think about work, what do you feel entitled to? Make a list of your perceived rights below.

____

____

____

____

____

____

____

Now ask yourself how you can reframe these perceived rights into an attitude of gratitude or the ability to perceive a fair exchange. Instead of an attitude of entitlement it would help you to focus on how you can close your performance gaps and take proactive steps to advance your career. If you are unable to detect your performance gaps or inappropriate behaviors, speak with an appropriate leader/coworker in a non-confrontational way so you can obtain authentic feedback.

____

____

____

____

____

____

____

Compile a list of things you can appreciate about your career, your coworkers, and your employer.

Self-Awareness Notes:

How are you truly perceived by others? (i.e. Are you entitled? Do you express appreciation toward or recognize your coworkers?) What do you plan to do differently to enhance your behavior?

E.Q. Librium Tip

Reward and recognition create opportunities to say *thank you*, but if the recognition happens in an environment where employees do not feel valued by leaders, the gesture is dismissed as insincere or meaningless.

BOUNDARY SETTING

BOUNDARIES are the parameters for behaviors that are acceptable at work. When managing your boundaries at the office, sometimes it will take multiple attempts to reinforce your boundaries because there are persons who have no boundaries, and they don't know how to adhere to anyone else's. Violation of boundaries can lead to low morale, reduced motivation, poor performance, over-worked employees, or disrespectful, belligerent staff.

Types of Boundary Violations

Indicate below the types of boundary issues you have experienced.

- Allowing other people's moods/attitudes to affect yours
- Difficulty expressing your needs
- Unable to say "no"
- Taking on responsibility inappropriately (when the responsibility is not yours, but you feel that it is, and you feel burdened by the responsibility)
- Bullying
- Persons with no boundaries who tend not to be aware of anyone else's boundaries
- Being treated unfairly
- Unclear role definition
- Unclear reporting lines
- Coworkers approaching you to borrow money
- Gossip
- Persons violating your space (searching your desk/accessing your computer, etc.)

Indicate how you may have violated other people's boundaries.

- Your tone (shouting/condescending, etc.)
- Your attitude
- Asking someone to do something that goes against his or her values
- Treating employees unfairly
- Gossip
- Asking persons to loan you money
- Impatience/rudeness
- Imposing your will on others

How to Set and Manage Your Boundaries

Boundaries are needed for functional work relationships to exist. When your boundaries are imposed upon or compromised, you can feel violated.

1. Negotiate deadlines.
2. Ask for what you need.
3. Establish your limits.
4. Constantly reinforce your limits, because people will test them despite your clarity.
5. Let people know the effect they have on you.
6. Ensure coworkers are communicating with you respectfully.
7. Do not divulge confidential information.
8. Avoid lending to or borrowing money from coworkers.
9. Do not participate in illegal behavior.
10. Respect your colleagues.
11. Don't attack coworkers through gossip.
12. Respectfully decline inappropriate requests. (that infringe on your values or breach policies and procedures or the law)

How will you manage your compromised boundaries in future?

____

____

____

____

____

____

____

____

What steps will you take to ensure you are not encroaching on your coworkers' boundaries in future?

Boundaries and Friendships at Work

As an emotionally intelligent colleague, another way to set boundaries is to learn the difference between being a friend and being friendly. Being a friend leads to sharing intimate private details about your life and socializing. Being friendly maintains the boundary of your private life and allows you to engage your coworkers authentically.

Working with friends can create a predicament if you have to make an unpopular decision. Whether you are fair with employees or not, they may assume you are discussing their situation with your friend. This is especially difficult when you are the manager and your friend is within your department.

There are times when you can work well with friends by defining clear boundaries together. If you don't, boundary infractions can lead to emotions including anxiety, anger, or frustration, and ultimately to deterioration in trust.

Here are a few steps you can take to create boundaries when working with friends:

1. Establish boundaries with close friends. Explain there will be a change in how you interact at work and what the change means.
2. Be fair in all your interactions.
3. Establish personal friendships outside the organization.
4. Avoid fraternizing inappropriately with your coworker friends.

Identify the friends you currently work with and how you plan to manage boundaries so you can maintain a reputation for fairness and professionalism.

Self-Awareness Notes:

How are you truly perceived by others? (i.e. What actions are you taking that may be construed as boundary infractions?) If change is needed, what do you plan to do differently?

____

____

____

____

____

____

____

____

____

____

____

____

____

____

____

E.Q. Librium Tip

Boundary setting is only the first step. Once set, you have to constantly maintain your boundaries, because invariably, someone will attempt to violate your established limits.

PERFECTIONISM

CONSTANTLY striving for perfection not only leads to toxic emotion within the perfectionist, but the people around the perfectionist are also subjected to pressure to attain perfection.

Characteristics of Perfectionists

1. You are hypercritical of yourself and others.
2. You are defensive when others criticize you.
3. You strive to be the best and you want the people around you to be the best.
4. You are more focused on the final goal than the process.
5. Others complain that the standards you set are too high.
6. You don't listen to other people's insights; you have all the answers.
7. You are impatient with others, frequently complaining about their incompetence.
8. You perceive someone with a different viewpoint as difficult.
9. You fear/or take steps to avoid failure.

Take time to reflect on whether or not you are a perfectionist. If so, what are your behaviors, and how are you affecting the people around you?

______

______

______

______

______

______

Managing Perfectionism

Here are a few tips you can consider to help yourself and others to overcome perfectionism. Select those that can work for you:

- Perceive the positive in situations.
    - See the perfection in imperfection.
    - See the learning opportunities in perceived failures.
    - Learn from critics.

- Alter your self-talk.
    - Recognize there is sometimes not one right way or one answer.
    - Work toward *excellence* instead of *perfection.*
    - Forgive yourself.
    - Avoid being driven by others' opinions.

- Engage in strategic thinking.
    - Define your goals.
    - Set a time limit. (Recognize how you are becoming less effective and efficient because of your perfectionism.)

Perfection vs. Excellence

Perfection is being right.

Excellence is being willing to be wrong.

Perfection is fear.

Excellence is taking a risk.

Perfection is anger and frustration.

Excellence is powerful.

Perfection is control.

Excellence is spontaneous.

Perfection is judgment.

Excellence is accepting.

Perfection is taking.

Excellence is giving.

Perfection is doubt.

Excellence is confidence.

Perfection is pressure.

Excellence is natural.

Perfection is the destination.

Excellence is the journey.

Reference: Frank Maguire, (the original Senior Vice President of Industrial Relations for FedEx.) in notes drafted while in a hospital.

If you are a perfectionist, what can you do differently to move from a standard of perfection to one of excellence?

___

___

___

___

___

___

___

___

___

___

___

If you are not a perfectionist but you are negatively affected by one, what can you do differently?

Favoritism

FAVORITISM occurs when you have people around you who are aligned with your value systems and related positive biases. They can do no wrong and if you are unconscious about your behaviors, you may demonstrate preferential treatment. Conversely, persons who are different from you may seem challenging to you, and your behaviors can range from avoidance to a more competitive approach in which you take a defensive posture.

Some managers unconsciously demonstrate favoritism because they just want to get the work done. For others, they just don't respect people who are different. When you have a positive bias, it is important for you to learn to adopt an inclusive approach where you are able to embrace people who are different from you, harnessing their viewpoints in a way that strengthens your relationships and your solutions.

If you don't learn how to demonstrate inclusive behavior, you can contribute to dynamics of a political work environment. By demonstrating inclusive behavior you change power structures within the workplace and set the stage for collaboration. The exercise below is designed to help you to identify your inclusive and exclusive behaviors so you can consciously modify them when necessary.

When deciding whether or not to demonstrate enhanced inclusive behaviors you have a few choices.

1. Reject persons who are different from you. You are going to maintain your beliefs and reject people who are different from you. This is exclusive behavior and it can create unhealthy dynamics.
2. Pretend to be inclusive. This is usually perceived by others as being fake and is largely ineffective.
3. Maintain your beliefs and change your behaviors. There are some value systems that you will not be prepared to change. If you decide to take this route, the reason for changing your behavior has to be authentic, otherwise your attempts to change will be perceived as insincere. For example, you may decide that you will treat all your coworkers with respect despite your disagreement with their values.
4. Challenge your beliefs and behaviors; remain open to authentic change.

Inclusion Exercise (Situational)

The next step is to do some introspection to identify your exclusive behaviors and move them to inclusivity.

Identify persons with whom you prefer to work.

Why do you prefer to work with these people? What are their positive attributes?

Think about whether or not you demonstrate preferential treatment and how you do this.

How can you reframe your views so you can move from favoritism to inclusive behavior?

Identify people at work whom you perceive to be difficult.

Why do you perceive these people as difficult? What are some of their qualities?

Think about whether or not you demonstrate discriminating treatment and record how you do this.

How can you reframe your views so you can move from discriminating to inclusive behavior?

Let Go of the Past

IF you have been working long enough, you have had both high and low points in your career. You can choose to let these experiences create patterns of favoritism or embitterment—or you can choose to grow from your past situations.

When an experience is perceived as negative, forgiveness is sometimes necessary to build and maintain healthy working relationships. A person who is able to forgive recognizes that no-one is perfect. They know that someone is bound to cross the line or let them down either unintentionally or intentionally.

When you are unable to let go of the past, whether the experience is positive or negative, you are unable to perceive the present realistically and you make decisions that are not driven by emotion.

Compile of list of situations in which you tend not to let go of the past, whether the experiences are positive or negative.

____

____

____

____

____

____

Self-Awareness Notes:

How are you truly perceived by others with regard to letting go of the past? Why do they perceive you this way? Are you capable of letting the past go or do you hold onto past injustices or successes? What do you plan to do differently to enhance your behavior?

____

____

____

____

____

____

The Blame Game

THERE are people who, when confronted, will blame others or circumstances. Some will manufacture excuses, and others won't acknowledge when there is an issue. Whatever the variation, each example is disingenuous, and they all seek to transfer or deflect blame or ownership.

Whether you are a leader or not, if you are looking to blame someone for a difficulty, understand that you are perpetuating an environment where there is a lack of trust and ownership. Sometimes you do this because you were blamed in the past, so it is time to break the cycle and identify the root causes of a current challenge. Then assign responsibility instead of blame. Talk about what or how instead of who.

On the other hand, it is important to give credit where it is due and not take credit—actively or passively—for anyone else's contributions.

It is important to note that blaming and accepting inappropriate credit are both patterns of low confidence. Both behaviors can indicate an inability to allow yourself to be seen in a negative light.

Tips for Moving From Blame to Responsibility

If you would like to take more responsibility, select the points below that can work for you.

- ***Deliver on your commitments.*** If you can't, at least provide an update before the due date.
- ***Face your fears.*** Whether it is your fear of failure, fear of the unknown, or the fear of taking on more responsibility—face the fear. If possible, find ways to collaborate with others to get the work done. Keep in mind that courage occurs when you have a fear of something and you proceed anyway.
- ***Be prepared.*** In the preparation process you are building your knowledge base through research. If you prepare you won't need to blame anyone in an effort to deflect attention from the fact that you are unprepared.
- ***Acknowledge your shortcomings without being defensive.*** Blame is a defense mechanism. So instead of rejecting responsibility, admit your shortcomings. Your coworkers will respect and trust you.
- ***Give credit where it is due.*** If you did not facilitate a positive outcome, give the credit to the right person. Visibly giving credit to the right person(s) shows that you don't have to make yourself look good all the time, and it builds respect for you.
- ***Understand the fact that life will throw curve balls.*** Curve balls are a part of the natural order of things. They are usually out of your control and unpredictable. Don't blame the curve ball. Take steps to correct course and navigate your emotion as well as the obstacle.

In evolving from blame to responsibility, you can monitor your patterns of self talk. Some examples of self-defeating patterns of self talk in the context of blame are:

1. I have no choice.
2. This always happens.
3. This never goes right.
4. I am powerless.
5. I have no control.
6. It is not my fault.
7. I want to put myself in a better position than my coworker(s).
8. Other____

Select the self talk patterns above that you tend to use most.

What are some of the reasons you use to justify assigning blame or taking credit for the work of others?

Self-Awareness Notes:

How are you truly perceived by others? Do you directly or indirectly blame others? (i.e. How would you perceive others with similar behavior?) If appropriate, what do you plan to do differently to transform your behavior?

Stress Management

As stress levels increase, so do performance and creativity levels (initially), but there comes a point of diminishing return at which, after stress exceeds a peak level and is sustained over time, performance and efficiency levels decline.

When stress is sustained, so are high levels of emotion (anger/anxiety/impatience) that can contribute to dysfunction within a team. Unless you have the skills needed to become a buffer and absorb the stress without transmitting it to coworkers, you are probably contributing to the problem.

The Transformation Path

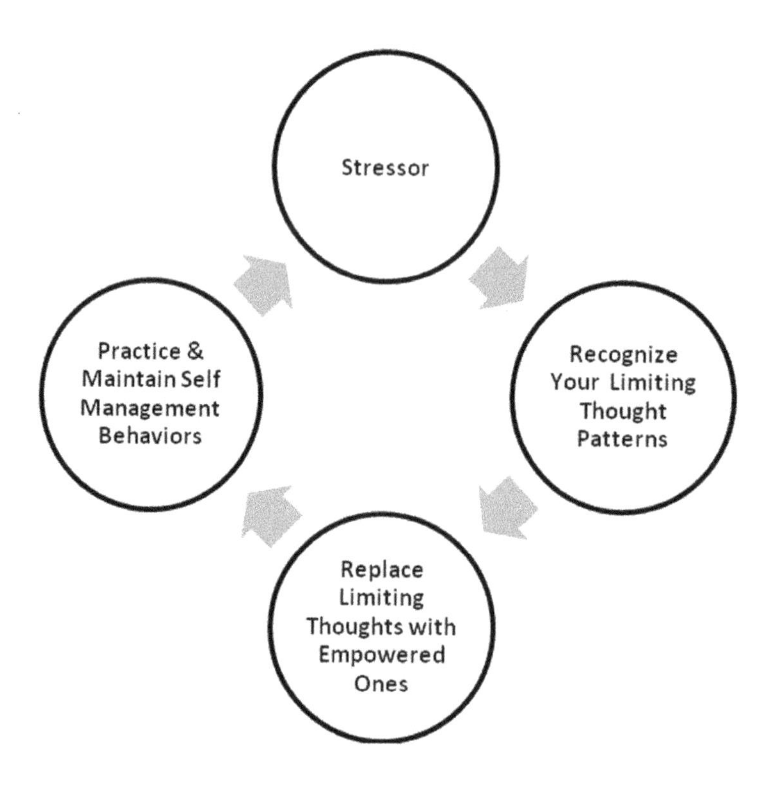

Here are a few tips to help you on the Stress Transformation Path.

Internal Actions	**External Actions**
Challenge your beliefs.	Find ways to relax: massages, down time, breathing exercises, laughter.
Forgive.	Exercise
Set boundaries. Learn how to say no constructively or learn how to renegotiate deadlines.	Take care of the stress-causing factor as soon as possible.
Focus on the positive/opportunity.	Organize your finances. Otherwise you will be preoccupied.
Rise above the hurt; seek objectivity.	Create a reliable system of follow-up.

Identify Your Stressors

The first step for managing your emotion when experiencing sustained stress is to identify the root causes of your internal stressors.

Identify your stressor(s) and the root causes.

Pay attention to what is occupying your mind and how it is affecting your mood.

Burn out occurs when you are psychologically exhausted over a period of time. When this occurs, it is typically difficult for you to motivate yourself. Focus on your general well-being. Are you burnt out? If so, why?

How does your stress manifest itself in your body?

Which emotions do you experience when you are in a state of stress?

Are your work relationships being affected by your stressed state? If yes, how are they affected? If no, check your understanding to ensure you are correct.

Develop a plan that will help you to address stressors. This plan is not only useful for balancing your emotional well-being, but your physical well-being will also be positively affected.

____

____

____

____

____

____

Self-Awareness Notes:

How are you truly perceived by others when you are in a stressed state? (balanced/apathetic/etc.) How can you determine whether your understanding of the impact of your stress on others is correct? If your impact is negative, what do you plan to do differently to enhance your behavior?

____

____

____

____

____

____

____

____

____

Politics at Work

POLITICAL dynamics within the workplace cause situations where persons attempt to create advantages for themselves through actual relationships or by projecting perceptions of beneficial relationships. Creating an advantage for yourself may mean creating a disadvantage for others and this typically puts you in a perceived position of power, because you have actively taken steps to elevate your status and gain a benefit that is not readily available to everyone. Here are different types of power you can encounter or exhibit at work.

Type of Power	Definition
Blocking	This refers to your tendency to block or disrupt the progress of a project, relationship, or system.
Expert	This type of power is used by persons who are subject-matter experts. They possess knowledge and experience that is valued and trusted.
Relationship	This is about your ability or perception of the ability to use certain relationships for personal advantages.
Appointed Position	This form of power comes from being appointed/hired to a position. Whether you are the right person for the role or not, you can use this type of power.
Elected Position	Elected position power comes from being elected by a majority vote.
Coercive	Coercive power is a type of power that refers to the ability to force an outcome that is desired for the person wielding the power and undesired for others.
Persuasive	This is the ability to influence people in a way that they believe or buy-into your view.
Resource	Resource power comes from owning or having control over resources that others need. This is directly connected to reward power where a person with reward power can bestow rewards once they have the resources.
Authentic	Power is authentic when it comes from being who you naturally are no matter what people think about you. You allow your uniqueness to shine. People around you may respect you for being who you are, but they may not necessarily like you.

Type of Power	Definition
Reward	This type of power is possessed by persons in authority who can decide who will be rewarded and who will not. They have the ability provide or withhold something determined to be of value.

References: French, J. R. P., Raven, B. *The Bases of Social Power*. In D. Cartwright and A. Zander. Group dynamics. New York: Harper & Row, (1959).

Shirts, Garry Ph.D. *Participant Guide for The Power of Leadership Simulation.* California: Simulation Training Systems, (2005) pp.33-34

Reflection

Using the list of power types, what types of power do you use that may create political dynamics at work? How often do you use each type of power?

Which types of power could you use but you choose not to wield?

Using the types of power list provided, which do type you typically encounter at work? Which do you participate in either by avoidance or active engagement?

Which emotions do you experience when you think about politics and the related power dynamics in the workplace? Why?

Jealous employees can group together and use blocking power to attempt to inhibit others. How have you tried to block your coworkers or how have coworkers tried to block you?

Typical Political Behaviors

Check those you use and place an "X" next to those you witness at work.

- Fixation on obtaining a promotion of status
- Manipulation
- Self-promotion
- Conflict (competitive behavior)
- Closed communication (only a few persons have information)
- Focus on form and image
- Gossip
- Sacrificing integrity to achieve a goal
- Decisions are made with more weight on relationships than on doing the right thing
- Closed agendas
- Demonstrating favoritism

Ways to Manage Office Politics with Integrity

Check those you already implement.

- Be aware of power structures. (Who is respected? Who can influence decisions?)
- Avoid making decisions without obtaining all the facts.
- Avoid taking sides, or displaying favoritism. Listen with objectivity despite your biases.
- Observe how your team responds to different political behaviors.
- Maintain your intrinsic motivation and integrity; don't sacrifice your personal values and ethics.
- Learn who influences decision making in your environment.
- Build the right relationships, the right way.
- Be confidential.
- Only say what can be repeated.
- Build your visibility (tastefully).
- Use charm or your ability to connect using vitality to persuade others. In the context of E.Q. Librium, your charismatic approach should also involve using integrity, sincerity, and trustworthiness.
- Avoid holding grudges or demonstrating vindictive behavior.

- Reduce uncertainty.
- Confront people who try to take advantage of others.
- Apply integrity to what you do.
- Resist gossip.
- When appropriate invite respected, influential persons to endorse you in the public domain. The point of this type of power is to convert non-believers into believers, providing legitimacy.
- Persons who set agendas control the topics covered, and depending on their facilitation skills, they can manage the scope of the conversation.

Values that inhibit you from engaging political office behaviors:

____

____

____

____

____

____

____

____

____

____

____

____

____

Many people shy away from engaging office politics. Power plays and allegiances are not of interest to them because they have labeled power as something inappropriate. What they do not understand is that whether or not they engage the political office games, they are already a part of a sometimes complex web of relationships. If you are in a situation like this and you are interested in maintaining your integrity, how can you engage in office politics without compromising your values? Use the list of *Ways to Manage Office Politics with Integrity* to formulate your response.

Self-Awareness Notes:

How political is your office environment? How political do you think you are? (i.e. How would you perceive others with similar behavior?) What do you plan to do differently to enhance your behavior and outcomes?

E.Q. Librium Tip

Politics within the workplace can be prolific and politics with integrity is very possible. Create a political style that does not cause you to contravene your personal value system.

Embracing Change

WHEN you are unable to step out of your comfort zone, you tend to resist change, viewing it as wrong or as a threat. Change could be threatening because you could stand to lose your status as a subject-matter expert, or because you fear you may not be able to do new work that is expected with similar skill, or there may be the possibility that you could be demoted or lose your job.

Once the change architects announce a change, there are three types of responses:

- Early adopters accept change early in the process. They embrace the vision with excitement and they can help to perpetuate positive views toward the change among their peers.
- Undecided persons are unclear about adopting the change. They take a wait-and-see approach and are unwilling to commit initially. Their emotions can be confusion, anger or anxiety. Display of these emotions can be tempered by the overwhelming need for job security.
- Persons who are a part of the change opposition resist any attempts to implement change. Resistant employees can experience emotions like anger, fear or resentment and if their deep emotions are addressed, they may become open to accepting the proposed change.

Over the years you may have taken each of these approaches to change initiatives at different times. Think about examples of each of your responses and where appropriate, consider what you can do differently.

What are the required circumstances for you to accept change? Which emotions are the most pronounced when you embrace change?

When you are undecided, what are usually your reasons? What are your related emotions? What does it take for you to accept the change?

When you oppose change, what are typically your reasons? What are your related emotions?

When you find yourself opposing change, how can you reframe the situation to evolve from a position of resistance?

____

____

____

____

____

____

Actions You Can Take When You or Your Coworkers Resist Change

- Explore the root causes. (your fears, concerns)
- Listen (without prejudice) to early adopters and change agents to understand their reasoning. Encourage them to share their point(s) of view.
- Share your views or fears in the right way, at the right time with the right people.
- Communicate often, creating top-down and bottom-up flows.
- Make constructive suggestions.
- Seek training or re-training where needed.
- Exercise flexibility with the process.
- Understand the needs and emotions of persons affected by the change.
- Help to build and maintain trust levels. Impaired trust helps no-one.

E.Q. Librium Tip

There are times when we resist change, and there are other times when we embrace it. Sometimes our value systems fuel our resistance, because values can be driven by the security of power structures or inefficient systems. Reflect on your vulnerabilities and develop yourself in those areas, because change is here to stay.

Self-Awareness Notes:

Which response to change do you typically deploy? (Early Adopter/Undecided/Resistor) Why? What do you plan to do differently to enhance your behavior?

PART THREE

CREATING YOUR E.Q. DEVELOPMENT PLAN

PART THREE is designed to help you to create a consolidated E.Q. Development plan so you can continue to build your emotional intelligence skills.

YOUR E.Q. DEVELOPMENT PLAN

NOW it is time to take all your commitments in this activity book and consolidate them into an action plan that will allow you to set goals for building your E.Q. and track them effectively.

STEP 1

What does your desired/future state of emotional self-management look like?

Your E.Q. S.W.O.T. (Strengths, Weaknesses, Opportunities and Threats) Analysis:

Use Your E.Q. Assessment Results

E.Q. Strengths (What are you good at?)	E.Q. Weaknesses (Where do you need to improve?)
Opportunities (For development)	**Threats (Obstacles to your development)**

STEP 2

Define Your Career Goals

Position/Area of Interest	E.Q. Competencies You Need to Develop (Use the E.Q. Competency List)

STEP 3

Define Your Other Goals

Financial/Social/Relationship/Health and Other Goals	E.Q. Competencies You Need to Develop (Use the E.Q. Competency List)

STEP 4

Your E.Q. Development Plan

1. **Objective:** Identify the E.Q. goal/outcome you would like to achieve.
2. **Success Criteria:** Define how you will recognize successful attainment of your goal.
3. **Developmental Actions:** What are the steps you need to take to meet your goal?
4. **Support:** Identify the people who can support you in your development through coaching, mentoring, providing feedback et cetera.
5. **Priority:** For the purpose of this exercise, there are three types of priorities: Identify your high, medium, and low priorities. Give some thought as to why you are assigning these priorities before assigning them.

Objectives	Success Criteria	Developmental Actions	Support	Priority
Which E.Q. competency or skill would I like to improve?	How will I define success?	Which methods will I use? (work-book, coaching, training, practice)	What role will others play in my development? (manager, peers, mentor, counselor, etc.)	High Medium Low

Objectives	Success Criteria	Developmental Actions	Support	Priority
Which E.Q. competency or skill would I like to improve?	How will I define success?	Which methods will I use? (workbook, coaching, training, practice)	What role will others play in my development? (manager, peers, mentor, counselor, etc.)	High Medium Low

Objectives	Success Criteria	Developmental Actions	Support	Priority
Which E.Q. competency or skill would I like to improve?	How will I define success?	Which methods will I use? (workbook, coaching, training, practice)	What role will others play in my development? (manager, peers, mentor, counselor, etc.)	High Medium Low

Objectives	Success Criteria	Developmental Actions	Support	Priority
Which E.Q. competency or skill would I like to improve?	How will I define success?	Which methods will I use? (work-book, coaching, training, practice)	What role will others play in my development? (manager, peers, mentor, counselor, etc.)	High Medium Low

Objectives	Success Criteria	Developmental Actions	Support	Priority
Which E.Q. competency or skill would I like to improve?	How will I define success?	Which methods will I use? (work-book, coaching, training, practice)	What role will others play in my development? (manager, peers, mentor, counselor, etc.)	High Medium Low

Objectives	Success Criteria	Developmental Actions	Support	Priority
Which E.Q. competency or skill would I like to improve?	How will I define success?	Which methods will I use? (work-book, coaching, training, practice)	What role will others play in my development? (manager, peers, mentor, counselor, etc.)	High Medium Low

Objectives	Success Criteria	Developmental Actions	Support	Priority
Which E.Q. competency or skill would I like to improve?	How will I define success?	Which methods will I use? (work-book, coaching, training, practice)	What role will others play in my development? (manager, peers, mentor, counselor, etc.)	High Medium Low

Sample E.Q. Development Plan Insertion

Objectives	Success Criteria	Developmental Actions	Support	Priority
Which E.Q. competency or skill would I like to improve?	How will I define success?	Which methods will I use? (workbook, coaching, training, practice)	What role will others play in my development? (manager, peers, mentor, counselor, etc.)	High Medium Low
Develop the ability to recognize and correct my behavioral patterns that are impeding the achievement of my career goals.	1) Improved ratings in the competency areas that are identified as opportunities for improvement 2) Propose stretch assignments to management to develop in weak areas. (Proposal to be submitted by: date) 3) Being promoted/ given additional responsibility within 1–2 years. 4) Able to read others' body language or nonverbal responses to determine when my pattern is not effective. 5) Achieve awareness of patterns. (set date)	Identification of my unproductive behavioral patterns through: 1) Talking to persons who will give me useful feedback. 2) Revisiting the behavioral pattern exercise 3) Coach 4) E.Q. Courses 5) Periodic measurement of my E.Q. 6) Practice 7) Obtain feedback during coaching and performance management discussions.	Speak with the following persons about my skill gaps and what they suggest I can do to address the gaps: 1) My current manager 2) My past managers 3) My peers 4) Obtain feedback from the HR department Once I obtain the initial feedback, set a date for a follow up conversation to determine whether the changes I made are perceivable.	High

People Who Can Support Your Development

MAKE a list of people who can support you in different aspects of your E.Q. Development plan. Select persons who are capable of giving you authentic, timely feedback that will foster your insight.

Name____

Email Address______________________________________

Phone contact information__________________Best time to call__________

How this person can help me___________________________

____

____

____

Name____

Email Address____

Phone contact information_____________________Best time to call__________

How this person can help me___________________________________

____

____

____

Name____

Email Address____

Phone contact information_____________________Best time to call__________

How this person can help me___________________________________

____

____

____

EMOTIONAL INTELLIGENCE COMPETENCIES

YOU can use this section as a tool to stimulate your thinking about what you would like to do differently.

Accountable Accountability refers to your ability to take responsibility for assigned tasks/work. It is an attitude of ownership that requires courage when you make mistakes that can cost your team or your organization.

Achievement Motivated This means you are capable of setting or adopting goals and executing plans with limited supervision or external motivating factors.

Active Listening Active listening refers to the ability to listen (using verbal and non-verbal communication skills). This type of listening involves, paraphrasing and probing to check understanding and skill at self-regulation so you allow a person to speak.

Adaptive Being adaptive involves the ability to display flexibility in new, ambiguous, and perceivably difficult circumstances.

Appreciative Showing appreciation refers to your capacity to thank employees for a job well done or going the extra mile. Appreciation can be systemic where there is a process integrated into policy or it can be natural. No matter the source, recognition should be well-timed and specific so the act of appreciation is meaningful to the person being recognized.

Attached Detachment This is the ability to prevent yourself from taking things personally while demonstrating empathy and accountability.

Aware of Power Structures This awareness is about the ability to identify, assess, and understand organizational power structures and engage them constructively, navigating limiting emotions and biases.

Both/And There are times we face choices, thinking we have to select one alternative. The Both/And skill is the ability to listen to and integrate more than one alternative into a solution. This lends itself to communicating a sense of inclusion and value.

Change Catalyst This characteristic means being capable of planning and initiating change. If change catalysts are not the architects of change, they are capable of grasping the vision and responding positively to the change initiators, becoming agents of change.

Coaching Feedback (Provides) Coaching feedback is developmental feedback that is not negatively critical in any way. It is supportive, constructive, engaging, and open. Employees receiving coaching feedback leave the session feeling inspired and motivated.

Communicative Being communicative involves providing the right information at the right time in the right way to the right people. Your coworkers are well-informed and the message transmission is ethical and developmental. You are also capable of listening to others without letting your biases set the tone.

Capable of Conflict Resolution This refers to your ability to identify and constructively resolve conflict, harnessing its developmental potential. It involves the application of conflict-resolution strategies, communication (listening) skills, and emotional intelligence.

Consequential Analysis Consequential analysis refers to your ability to identify and contemplate the consequences of various actions/scenarios, so you can weigh the risks and opportunities and make an optimal decision.

Creates Safe Space Creating safe space entails creating a work environment where employees feel comfortable sharing constructive criticism and recognition without fear of negative consequences. Safe space is respectful, constructive, and is characterized by curiosity.

Customer Oriented An emotionally intelligent employee recognizes the importance of ensuring that the customer receives a positive experience. Customer-focused employees recognize they are a part of the brand and make every effort to focus on the needs of customers. They also understand the importance of treating internal customers with respect and the same level of urgency as external customers, because they understand the consequences of inappropriate action/inaction.

Developer of Others Emotionally intelligent persons understand how to develop others whether they are peers, direct reports, or reporting managers/executives. They can identify skill gaps and assist with closing those gaps without making anyone feel deficient.

Diversity Conscious Many of us construe differences as difficult or challenging based on our biases. Diversity can add to the performance of a team if the creative tension is harnessed constructively, before it degenerates into counterproductive behavior based on stereotypes and prejudice. Without diversity-conscious behavior, teams are challenged to remain engaged, cohesive, and optimally operational.

Emotionally Literate Recognizing your emotions when they are happening is only one aspect of emotional literacy. It refers to the ability to identify and name both complex and simple emotional experiences. An emotionally-literate person is adept at naming multiple, coexistent emotions that may be contradictory or similar.

Empathetic Empathy is often viewed as the ability to put yourself in other people's shoes so you aren't judging them. Instead, empathy allows you to connect at a visceral level because you have had a similar experience.

Inclusive Inclusion is not always easy because we all have positive and negative biases that create division instead of diversity consciousness. Inclusivity is about being able to connect with people who are both the same and different. If persons around you are different inclusivity is about being able to connect with and engage them in a constructive way, despite their differences.

Initiative (Takes) You take initiative when you care. You don't wait to be instructed; you perceive a need and you take steps to resolve the need.

Intrinsically Motivated This skill is related to your ability to remain true to your values, mission, purpose, and goals in spite of external pressure.

Open to Others' Ideas When you listen to someone, it doesn't mean you are compelled to agree with that person, it means you are able to suspend your judgment, respect the diverse ideas, and collaborate.

Persuasive Persuasion refers to your ability to influence a change in someone else's thinking by using logic to appeal to values, beliefs, and/or emotion.

Politically Aware This happens when you are aware of all the power structures within your organization, and you develop the skills you need to navigate them without compromising your values.

Recognizes Emotional Patterns Behavioral patterns are sometimes imperceptible by the person demonstrating the behaviors. Unfortunately, everyone else is able to identify the patterns, react to them, or worse, manipulate you because your patterns are predictable.

Reframe This is about your ability to change your cognitive or emotional perspective by placing it in a different framework that both aligns with the facts and changes the meaning.

Resourceful This is the ability to make things happen despite the perceived lack of resources. Resourceful people can overcome their fears or perception of lack and become creative.

Responsible Honesty (Able to demonstrate) This is the ability to provide honest feedback that is constructive and developmental rather than blunt, scathing, or irresponsible, creating negative workplace dynamics or low morale because of fear or anger.

Right Timing (Capable of) When you suspend your judgment you are able to put your biases aside and make decisions, listen, and demonstrate inclusive behaviors that are based on rationale and balance, not emotion. Right timing refers to your ability to identify the right time to disclose, take action, or demonstrate emotion. The practice of right timing requires self-regulation because it takes patience to wait until the right time to divulge information or take action.

Self-Actualized You are motivated to achieve your full potential. You understand yourself and possess the internal drive necessary to continuously develop yourself.

Self-Aware Self-awareness refers to your ability to understand your emotions, but it also refers to your ability to understand how others perceive your behaviors.

Self-Regulated You are able to self regulate when you are in an emotional state and able to manage your reactions, and channel the emotion into a balanced outcome.

Solution driven This dynamic occurs when you possess an ability to review an ambiguous situation, create a plan, and execute the planned objectives. It is also applicable to informal discussions in which you are presented with a problem and you understand the consequences of not perceiving and creating a solution. Therefore, you close every conversation that requires this close with the words, "So what are your next steps?"

Suspending Judgment (Capable of) When you suspend your judgment you are able to put your biases aside and make decisions, listen, and demonstrate inclusive behaviors that are based on rationale and balance, not emotion.

Team Builder Requires the ability to build team competence, manage your emotions, resolve conflict and meet or exceed goals. It requires understanding individual motivations and talents. Team building also involves the ability to create synergies that can lead to creativity and high performance. It also requires the wisdom to determine when a team member is not a good fit and the ability to make a decision that may be difficult.

Transparent Transparence is not about being open about everything. It is about knowing what to say, how much of it to say, and when to say it. It helps to build trust and develop members of the team, because they are put in a position to be able to serve customers in the absence of subject-matter experts. Transparence brings clarity and it helps everyone to see the whole picture, motives, and rationale, to the extent possible.

PART FOUR

YOUR JOURNAL OF TRANSFORMATION

PART FOUR is designed to help you to work through your emotions by journaling.

Getting to E.Q. Librium Journal

THIS journal can be used for short notes to record your emotions on a daily basis, to track your emotional trends, or to explore particularly significant events that have had a deep, emotional impact on you.

BIBLIOGRAPHY

Baldridge, J.V. (1971). *Power and Conflict in the University.* New York: Wiley.

Bethel, Y.R. (2012). E.Q. Librium: *Unleash the Power of Your Emotional Intelligence: A Proven Path to Career Success.* Bahamas: Organizational Soul Ltd.

Estroff Marano, Hara (2008). *A Nation of Wimps.* New York: Broadway Books.

French, J.R.P., and Raven, B. (1959). The bases of social power. In D. Cartwright and A. Zander (Eds.), *Group Dynamics.* New York: Harper & Row.

Hackman, M.A., and Johnson, C.E. (1991). *Leadership: A Communication Perspective.* Prospect Heights, IL: Waveland Press.

Kanter, R.M. (1977). *Men and Women of the Corporation.* New York: Basic Books.

King, A. (1987). *Power & Communication.* Prospect Heights, IL: Waveland Press.

Parrott, W. (2001), *Emotions in Social Psychology.* Psychology Press, Philadelphia.

Plutchik, Robert (1980), *Emotion: Theory, research, and experience: Vol. 1. Theories of emotion,* **1**, New York: Academic

Six Seconds Emotional Intelligence website and blog, http://*www.6seconds.org*

Unlock your potential.

Experience your career and your life like never before.

Understand yourself and others.

Improve your work relationships.

Become a better leader.

The E.Q. Effect

Discover products and services designed to enhance your emotional intelligence.

- *E.Q. Librium: Unleash the Power of your Emotional Intelligence, A Proven Path to Career Success*, provides you with practical, proven tips that will help you to navigate your emotions when faced with challenging circumstances at work. It complements the Activity Book, Getting to E.Q. Librium, providing effective theory and tools that help you to self-develop.

- *Getting To E.Q. Librium* is an introspective activity book that can benefit employees at all levels within an organization. The activities are short yet effective.

- *The Games People Play at Work* is an interactive, single outcome simulation that helps learners to get into the habits of identifying their emotions and consistently making emotionally-competent decisions.

- *The E.Q. Effect Learning Paths* are practical, tested tools that will improve E.Q. at both an organizational and individual level. The learning paths are introspective and interactive, using *E.Q. Mastery Groups* to sustain emotionally competent behavior over time.

- *Change Management* is an integral part of the E.Q. transformation process. We provide a variety of tools designed to stimulate and measure change. Our aim is to create and sustain the desired E.Q. state.

To learn more about available E.Q. tools you can visit www.theeqeffect.com.

About the Author

As an author, E.Q. specialist, consultant, trainer, and speaker, Yvette Bethel understands the inner working of organizations and how to effectively bring together the corporate vision of business with the know-how of the staff. She encourages personal and professional growth and healthy working relationships.

Bethel is a Fulbright Scholar who put her acquired skills to good use with over twenty years' experience in the banking industry prior to launching an HR consulting and training business. During her tenure in the banking industry, she served in senior capacities in customer service, operations, corporate strategy, marketing, PR, training, and human resources. Bethel's HR and training experience commenced in the late 1980s, and in her last HR and training role, Bethel's portfolio included a group of eight Caribbean countries.

Possessing international exposure in the areas of human resources and training, Bethel continually seeks to integrate this experience with her emotional intelligence expertise. She is a member of an international emotional intelligence network called Six Seconds, and this connects her with an E.Q. community that spans the globe.

In her enthusiasm for improving emotional intelligence in the workplace, Bethel developed multiple learning tools, specially designed to bring about E.Q. change for individuals and organizations. Bethel is the author of: the CD audio book, ***Your Workplace Survival Kit***; book, ***E.Q. Librium, Unleash the Power of Your Emotional Intelligence: A Proven Path to Career Success***; and activity book, ***Getting to E.Q. Librium***. She is also the author of the E.Q. simulation, ***The Games People Play at Work***.

www.theeqeffect.com.

Lightning Source UK Ltd.
Milton Keynes UK
UKHW032231200220
359047UK00008BB/766